Build Studio Light Setup using 3ds Max® and VRay®

Raavi O'Connor

Build Studio Light Setup using 3ds Max and VRay

Book Code: V002C

ISBN: 978-1515196105

http://raavidesign.blogspot.co.uk

Contents

This page is intentionally left blank

Acknowledgements

Thanks to:

Sarah O'Connor for the cover art and other promotional material.
Alex for formatting the book.
Everyone at Autodesk [www.autodesk.com].
Everyone at Chaos Group [www.chaosgroup.com].

Thanks to all great digital artists who inspire us with their innovative VFX, gaming, animation, and motion graphics content.

And a very special thanks to everyone who helped me along the way in my life and carrier.

Finally, thank you for picking up the book.

This page is intentionally left blank

About the Author

Raavi Design, founded by Raavi O'Connor, is a group of like-minded professionals and freelancers who are specialized in advertising, graphic design, web design and development, digital marketing, multimedia, exhibition, print design, branding, and CG content creation.

At Raavi Design we strive to share the enthusiasm and ideas with other digital artists and provide quality CG content to the aspiring artists and students. Our books are written in an easy to understand language so that the users learn the complex concepts quickly.

The main features of our books are as follows:

- Nicely formatted content in books
- Less theory more practical approach saves you hours of struggle and pain
- Content written in easy to understand language
- Exercises/Labs for practice
- Free updates and exclusive bonus content
- Video tutorials
- Free textures, background design, and 3D files

Here's the list of training books that Raavi has put together:

- The Tutorial Bank: 3D, VFX, & Motion Graphics
- Build Studio Light Setup using 3ds Max and VRay
- Exploring Standard Materials in 3ds Max 2015
- Exploring Standard Materials in 3ds Max 2016
- Exploring Utilities Nodes In Maya 2016 [Coming Soon]
- Create Backgrounds, Textures, and Maps in Photoshop: Using Photoshop CC 2014
- Beginner's Guide To Mental Ray and Autodesk Materials In 3ds Max 2016
- Beginner's Guide For Creating 3D Models In 3ds Max 2016 [Coming Soon]

You can follow **Raavi O'Conner** on twitter **@raavidesign**.

This page is intentionally left blank

Book Overview

This eBook will help you to create your own custom studio light setup using 3ds Max and VRay. This books is written for a broad set of users but it assumes that you have the basic knowledge of 3ds Max and VRay. The hands-on exercise in this book is created using 3ds Max 2014 and VRay 3.0.

Topics covered in this book:

- Creating environment for the studio light setup using the **Syke** plugin.
- Setting units for the studio setup.
- Using the exposure controls of the **VRay Physical Camera**.
- Creating chrome shader using **VRay Material**.
- Setting **VRay Lights** to illuminate the setup.
- Specifying the test and final settings for the **VRay Renderer**.
- Using the **Linear** workflow.

* Visit http://bit.ly/studio-light for more info.

What you need?

To complete the hands-on exercise in this book, you need v2014 of Autodesk 3ds Max and v3.0 of VRay. To know more about these products from Autodesk, visit the following links:

3ds Max: *http://www.autodesk.com/products/3ds-max/overview*

If you are an educator or student, you can access free Autodesk software from the **Autodesk Education Community**. The **Autodesk Education Community** is an online resource with more than five million members that lets educators and students to download free Autodesk software. In addition, you can connect with millions of other digital artists to know about latest and greatest happening in the CG industry.

Resources

This book is sold via multiple sales channels. If you don't have access to the resources used in this book, you can place a request for the resources by visiting the following link: *http://bit.ly/rd-contact*. Please mention **"Resources - V002C"** in the subject line.

Customer Support

At Raavi Design we believe support is personal. Our technical team is always ready to take care of your technical queries. If you face any problem with the technical aspect of the book, navigate to *http://bit.ly/rd-contact* and let us know about your query. Please mention **"Technical Query - V002C"** in the subject line. We will do our best to resolve your queries.

Reader Feedback

Your feedback is always welcome. Your feedback is critical to our efforts at Raavi Design and it will help us in developing quality titles in the future. To send the feedback, visit *http://bit.ly/rd-contact*. Please mention **"Feedback - V002C"** in the subject line.

Build Studio Light Setup using 3ds Max and Vray

The key to render nice and clean product visuals using 3ds Max and VRay is to setup a clean studio environment. You can use a drag and drop environment such as **HDR Light Studio** to create these visuals. However, if you want to make your product shots different from others, you need to create your own custom studio setup. In the hands-on exercise, I will describe one of the method to creates studio lighting setup.

eBook overview

This eBook will help you to create your own custom studio light setup using 3ds Max and VRay. This eBook is written for a broad set of users but it assumes that you have the basic knowledge of 3ds Max and VRay. The tutorial in this eBook is created using 3ds Max 2014 and VRay 3.0. Topics covered in this eBook are as follows:

- Creating environment for the studio light setup using the **Syke** plugin
- Setting units for the studio setup
- Using the exposure controls of the **VRay Physical Camera**
- Creating chrome shader using **VRay Material**
- Setting **VRay Lights** to illuminate the setup
- Specifying the test and final settings for the **VRay Renderer**
- Using the **Linear** workflow

Creating VRay Studio Light Setup

You will first create a background environment and then illuminate the scenes using VRay lights. You will also create the test and final render presets for rendering the test and final results, respectively.

Specifying the Units for the Project

To get the realistic results using VRay it is must that you use the correct scale settings while modeling the scene. Let's set the scene units to **Centimeters**.

From the **Customize** menu, choose **Units Setup**. In the **Units Setup** dialog that appears, choose **Metric** from the **Display Unit Scale** group. Next, choose **Centimeters** from the drop-down located below **Metric**, if not already chosen. Click **OK** to accept the changes. RMB click on any snap toggle button on the **Main** toolbar. In the **Grid and Snap Settings** dialog that opens, choose **Home Grid** and then set **Grid Spacing** to **5**, **Major Lines every Nth Grid Line** to **5**, and **Perspective View Grid Extent** to **8**. Close the **Grid and Snap Settings** dialog. Save the scene with the name **studioSetup.max**.

Setting Gamma

A computer monitor is a nonlinear device. The difference in actual luminance values does change with value stored in it. The gamma correction compensate for this nonlinearity of computer displays and image file formats. If a render image calculated using linear data is displayed directly on the computer monitor, the image will not match what it would look like under real-world conditions (lit by real lights, viewed by real eyes). This mismatch is compensated using the **Gamma Correction**.

Note: Formula used for the Gamma calculations
The formula used for the gamma calculation is output_intensity = input_intensity (1/gamma). It is evident from the formula that if you set gamma to 1, the image would not be adjusted at all.

Note: Gamma 2.2 and linear workflow
To know more about gamma 2.2 and linear workflow in 3ds Max, visit the following link:
http://bit.ly/linear-gamma.

Choose Preferences from the Customize menu to open the Preferences dialog. In this dialog, go to the **Gamma and LUT** tab and then make sure **Gamma** is chosen in the **Display** group and **Gamma** is set to **2.2**. Also, make sure **Affect Color Selectors** and **Affect Material Editor** are on. Click **OK**.

Specifying the Renderer

Here, you will set the renderer as VRay as well as set the output size for the rendered output.

Click **Render Setup** from the **Main** toolbar to open the **Render Setup** dialog. On the **Common tab | Assign Renderer rollout**, click **Choose Renderer**. In the **Choose Renderer** dialog that opens, select **V-Ray Adv** and then click **OK**. On the **Common panel | Output Size rollout**, choose **Custom** from the drop-down and then set **Width** to **300** and **Height** to **375**. Now, click **Image Aspect's** lock button. Close the **Render Setup** dialog.

Specifying Test Settings for VRay

Now, let's set the test settings for the **VRay** renderer. To test the illumination in the scene, you need to set up the **VRay** renderer with low values. These low value will allow us to quickly view the illumination.

Click **Render Setup** from the **Main** toolbar to open the **Render Setup** dialog. Go to the **V-Ray** tab. On the **Image sampler (Antialiasing)** rollout, turn off **Image filter**.

Turning off **Image filter** disables the algorithm used for sampling and filtering the image function. I switched it off to produce quick results. I will switch it on again during the final image rendering process.

On the **Global DMC** rollout, set **Adaptive amount** to **1.0** and **Noise threshold** to **0.016**.

The **Monte Carlo** sampling is a method for evaluating "blurry" values such as antialiasing, reflections/refractions, translucency, and so forth. VRay uses a variant of **Monte Carlo** called **DMC (Deterministic Monte Carlo)**. Unlike the **Mote Carlo** sampling that uses different pseudo-random numbers for samples, DMC uses a pre-defined set of samples thus allowing you to reduce the noise. The controls in the **Global DMC** rollout allow you to specify settings for the **DMC** sampler.

Adaptive amount controls the extent to which the number of samples depends on the blurry values that DMC calculates. A value of **1** means that full adoption of the blurry values. **Noise threshold** controls when a blurry value is good enough to be used.

On the **Environment** rollout, turn on **GI environment** and set **color** to **white**. Also, turn on **Reflection/refraction environment**.

The controls in the **Environment** rollout allow you to override the 3ds Max's environment settings for indirect illumination. You can specify a color and a texture map (HDRI) to be used during GI and reflection/refraction calculations.

On the **Color mapping** rollout, set **Type** to **HSV Exponential** and make sure **Gamma** is set to **2.2**. Also, enable **Sub-pixel** mapping.

The controls in this rollout allow you to set the rendering exposure and gamma correction. The default **Reinhard** algorithm is a hybrid algorithm. It is combination of other two algorithms: **Exponential** and **Linear**. This algorithm allows you to create rich and vibrant images. The **Exponential** type controls the saturation of the colors based on their brightness. It helps in reducing the burnouts in bright areas. It clamps the colors so that no value exceeds **255** or **1** in the floating point value. The **HSV Exponential** type is similar to the **Exponential** type but it prevents the washing out of the color towards white. It preserves the color hue and saturation.

The **Gamma** controls let you perform gamma correction on the image. I have set **Gamma** to **2.2** in the preferences, therefore, make sure that **Gamma** in the **Color** mapping rollout is also set to **2.2**. **Sub-pixel mapping** control allows you to specifiy whether color mapping will be applied to the final image pixels or to the individual sub-pixel samples.

Go to the **GI** tab and then in the **Global illumination** rollout, turn on **Enable GI**. Set **Secondary engine** to **Light cache**.

The controls in the **Global Illumination** rollout specify an algorithm for computing indirect illumination. In this rollout, you can specify a GI engine for calculating primary and secondary bounces. **Irradiance map** works on the irradiance caching. The indirect illumination is calculated at some points in the scene and interpolate for rest of the scene. The **Light cache** engine approximates the global illumination in the scene by using a light map. The light map is built by tracing eye paths from the camera. Each path or ray stores the illumination from the rest of the paths into a 3d structure. The Light cache can be used both for interior and exterior scenes.

On the **Irradiance map** rollout, set **Current preset** to **Very low**, and **Subdivs** to **30**. On the **Light cache** rollout, set **Subdivs** to **350**.

The **Current preset** drop-down lets you select a preset for the irradiance map parameters. The **Very low** preset can be used for preview purpose, it shows general lighting in the scene. **Subdivs** is responsible for the quality of individual GI samples. Higher values produce smooth results but tax you on the render time.

The **Subdivs** control in the **Light cache** rollout is responsible for number of paths to be traced from the camera. I have specified a value of **350** for this control which effectively produces **122500** (the square of the Subdivs) paths.

Go to the **Settings** tab and then in the **System** rollout, set **Bucket width** to **16**.

Buckets are rendering regions in VRay which is a rectangular part of the currently rendered frame that is rendered independently from other buckets.

Go to the **Common** tab and then choose **Save Preset** from the **Preset** drop-down. In the **Render Presets Save** dialog that opens, navigate to the location when you want to save the render preset. Type the **testPreset** in the **File name** type-in box and then click **Save**. In the **Select Preset Categories** dialog that opens, make sure all categories are selected and then click **Save** to save the preset. Close the **Render Setup** dialog.

Creating the Backdrop

Now, you need to create a backdrop for the product. There are many techniques to create a backdrop in 3ds Max. However, here you will use a free plugin **Syke** developed by **JokerMartini**. You can download the plugin from the following link: *http://jokermartini. com/syke*.

Navigate to *http://jokermartini.com/syke* and download the script. Now, run the script. The **Syke** button gets displayed in the **Create panel | Geometry | Standard Primitives | Object Type rollout** [see Figure 1]. Create a **Syke** in the **Top** viewport. Now, go to the **Modify** panel and then set **Width** to **0**, **Depth** to **500**, **Height** to **400**, **Radius** to **95**, **Width Segs** to **24**, **Depth Segs** to **6**, **Height Segs** to **6**, **Radius Segs** to **6**. Make sure **Alignment** is set to **Center**.

Set **Bend Amount** to **180**, and **Bend Direction** to **90**. Figure 2 shows the **Syke** in viewports. Rename **Syke** as **backdropGeo**. Go to the **Create** panel, click **Geometry | Extended Primitives**, then click **TorusKnot**. In the **Top** viewport, create a knot. Rename the knot as **torusGeo**.

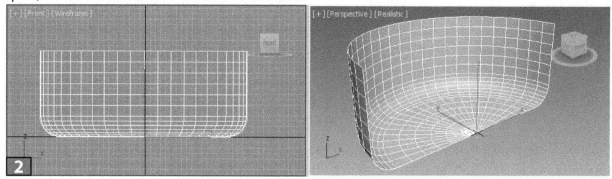

On the **Modify panel | Parameters rollout | Base Curve group**, set **Radius** to **58** and **Segments** to **200**. In the **Cross Section** group, set **Radius** to **25**. Now, align the **torusGeo** [see Figure 3]. Press **Ctrl+S** to save the scene.

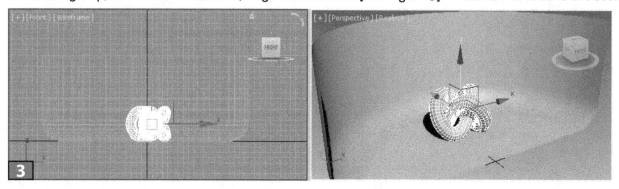

Creating the Camera

Now, let's add a **VRay Physical Camera**. This camera lets you use the real-world parameters such as f-stop, focal length of the lens, and shutter speed to set up the virtual CG camera. These camera attributes give you greater control on the exposure level.

Go to the **Create** panel, click **Cameras | VRay**, then click **VRayPhysicalCam**. In the **Top** viewport, create a camera and then rename the camera as **vrayCam**. Activate the **Perspective** viewport and then press **C** to switch to the camera view. Next, press **Shift+F** to show safe frames. Now, adjust the camera view [see Figure 4].

Press **F9** to take a test render [see Figure 5]. You will see that the render is dark. Let's adjust the camera exposure attributes to make scene bright. Select **vrayCam** in a viewport and then on the **Modify panel | Basic parameters rollout**, select **Temperature** from the **white balance** drop-down. Set **temperature** to **5500**, **f-number** to **6**, and **shutter speed** to **20**. Press **F9** to take a test render (figure 6). You can now clearly see difference these values made in the render shown in Figure 6.

The **f-number** control is responsible for changing the width of the camera aperture which in-turn adjusts the exposure. If **Exposure** is turned on, changing **f-number** value affects the brightness of the image. The **white balance** drop-down allows you to specify a color. The objects in the scene that have the specified color will appear white in the image. Only hue of the color is taken into consideration and brightness of the color is ignored. If you choose **Temperature** from this drop-down, you can specify the temperate of the color using the **temperate** control. The **shutter speed** is the speed of shutter of the still photographic camera in inverse seconds. Lower shutter speed makes images brighter.

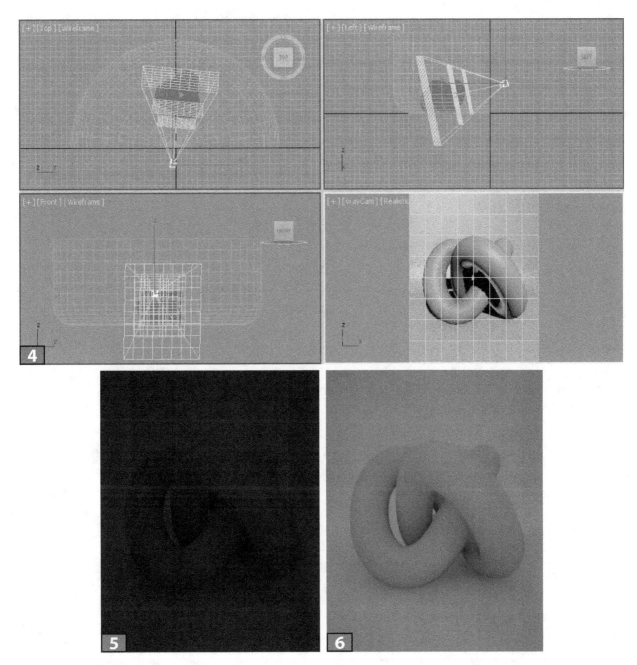

Creating Materials

Here, I will create materials for the backdrop and torus. I will use the **Standard** VRay material to create materials for the environment and torus in the scene. For the torus, I will create chrome material using the **Falloff** standard map.

Press **M** to open the **Slate Material Editor**. On the **Material/Map Browser | Materials | V-Ray rollout**, double-click **VRayMtl**. Rename the material as **backdropMat** and assign it to the **backdropGeo**. On the **Parameter Editor | Basic Parameters rollout | Diffuse group**, click **Diffuse** color swatch. In the **Color Selector: diffuse** dialog that opens, set **Value** to **223** and click **OK**.

Now, you will create a material for the **torusGeo**.

Add another **VRayMtl** and rename it as **torusMat**. Assign **torusMat** to **torusGeo**. Double-click on **torusMat** to display its parameters. On the **Parameter Editor | Basic parameters rollout | Diffuse group**, click **Diffuse** color swatch. In the **Color Selector: diffuse** dialog that opens, set **Value** to **2** and click **OK**. Drag the **Reflect** map socket of **torusMat** to the empty area of the active view. In the popup menu that appears [see Figure 7], select **Standard > Falloff** to connect a **Falloff** map to the **Reflect** map of **torusMat** [see Figure 8]. Double-click on the **Falloff map** node. On the **Parameter Editor | Falloff parameters rollout > Front : Side group**, change the color of the black color swatch to white. Click on the bottom white color swatch to open the **Color Selector: Color 2** dialog. Set **Value** to **240** in this dialog and click **OK**. Set **Falloff Type** to **Fresnel**.

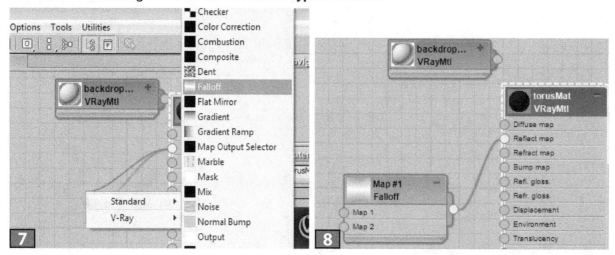

On the **torusMat | Parameter Editor | Basic parameters rollout | Reflection** group, clear **Fresnel reflections**. Set **Refl. glossiness** to **0.9** and **Subdivs** to **16**. Now, take a test render by pressing **F9** [refer Figure 9].

Illuminating the Scene

Now, let's add some VRay lights to brighten the scene. We will use three VRay lights with different strength, power, and colors. I will use the **Temperature** control to set the color of the light.

Go to the **Create** panel, click **Lights | VRay**, then click **VRayLight**. In the **Front** viewport, create a light. Rename the light as **leftLight**. Align the **leftLight** [see Figure 10]. You can also use the following values for aligning **leftLight**:

Transform (X, Y, Z): -289.425, 99.69, 190.906
Rotation (X, Y, Z): 90, 0, -43.497

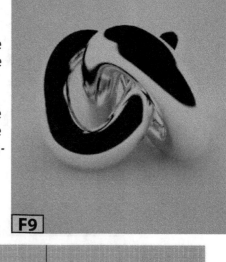

F9

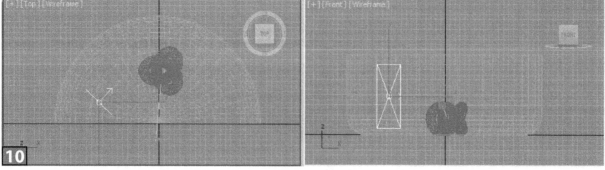

VRayLight is a **VRay** specific light source plugin that allows you to create physically accurate area lights.

Go to the **Modify** panel, on the **Parameters rollout | Intensity group**, set **Units** to **Radiant Power (W)**, **Multiplier** to **100**, **Mode** to **Temperature**, and **Temperature** to **5500**. Take a test render [see Figure 11].

When you use **Radiant Power** the intensity of light does not depend on its size. **Radiant Power** measures the total emitted power in **watts**. This is not the same as the power consumed by an electric bulb. A **100W** light bulb emits **2** to **3** watts as visible light. **Multiplier** is the multiplier for the color of the light. **Temperature** sets the color emitted by the light.

On the **Sampling** group set **Subdivs** to **24**.

The **Subdivs** value controls the number of samples used to compute the lighting. Higher values produce smooth results but take more time to render.

Create another V-Ray light with the name **rightLight** and place it opposite of **leftLight** [see Figure 12]. You can use the following coordinates for aligning the light:

Transform: 302.242, 123.309, 190.906
Rotation: 90.0, 0.0, 71.567

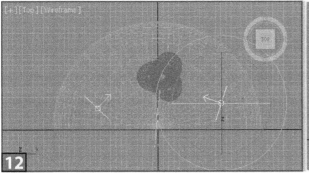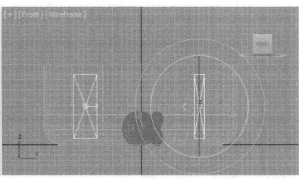

Go to the **Modify** panel, on the **Parameters rollout | Intensity** group, set **Units** to **Radiant Power (W)**, **Multiplier** to **80**, **Mode** to **Temperature**, and **Temperature** to **5500**. On the **Sampling** group set **Subdivs** to **24**. Now, take a test render [see Figure 13]. Create another V-Ray light with the name **topLight** in the **Top** viewport and place it as shown in Figure 14. You can also use the following coordinates:

Transform: -4.187, 241.668, 331.037
Rotation: 0, 0, 0

Go to the **Modify** panel, on the **Parameters rollout | Intensity group**, set **Units** to **Radiant Power (W)**, **Multiplier** to **60**, **Mode** to **Temperature**, and **Temperature** to **5000**. On the **Sampling** group set **Subdivs** to **24**. Now, take a test render by pressing **F9** [see Figure 15]. Now, let's boost the strength of all lights to illuminate the scene evenly. Select **leftLight** in a viewport and then on the **Modify panel | Intensity group**, set **Multiplier** to **170**. Similarly, set **Intensity** to **120** and **90** for **rightLight** and **topLight**, respectively. Take a test render [see Figure 16].

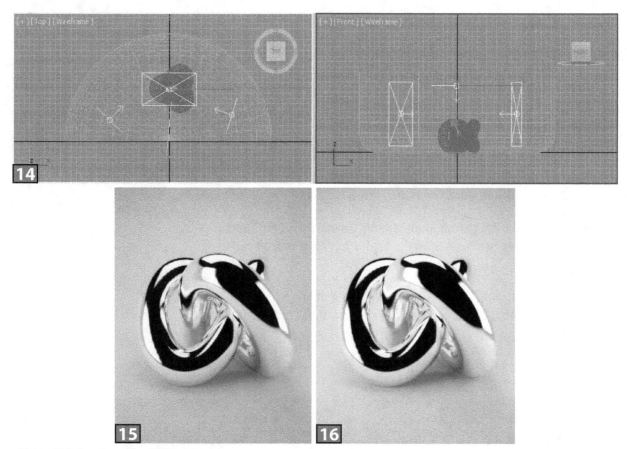

Specifying HQ Settings for VRay

The lighting is looking good now. Let's set the high quality settings for the renderer to get a high quality render.

Click **Render Setup** from the **Main** toolbar to open the **Render Setup** dialog. Go to the **V-Ray** tab. On the **Image sampler (Antialiasing)** rollout, enable **Image** filter. Set **Filter** to **Mitchell-Netravali** and **Blur** to **0.25**.

The **Type** is set to **Adaptive** that considers a variable number of samples per pixel based on the difference in the intensity of the pixels. **Mitchell-Netravali** is an antialiasing filter applied to the final result. This process is different than rendering an image without filter and then blurring the image using a post application such as **Adobe Photoshop**. Applying filter at the render time produces a much more accurate result. The **Mitchell-Netravali** filter lets you control the edge enhancement and blurring. **Blur** lets you control the blurriness.

On the **Adaptive** image sampler rollout, set **Max subdivs** to **10**. Turn off **Use DMC sampler thresh.** and then set **Color threshold** to **0.001**.

The **Adaptive sampler** can be used if your want to render an image that has lot of details. It also takes less RAM than the **Adaptive subdivision sampler**. The **Min subdivs** control lets you determine the minimum number of samples taken for each pixel. Generally, you should keep the **Min subdivs** vale to **1**. Increase this value if there are very thin line in the image or you are rendering a scene with fast moving objects and you are using the motion blur. The actual number of pixels are square of this number. **Max subdivs** is responsible for the maximum number of samples for a pixel.

When **Use DMC sampler threshold** is on, the threshold value specified in the **DMC sampler** rollout is used to determine if more samples are needed for a pixel. If turned off, the **Color threshold** value is used.

On the **Global DMC** rollout, set **Adaptive amount** to **0.85**, **Noise threshold** to **0.001**, and **Min samples** to **16**.

In adaptive sampling (also known as early termination), when the samples are taken and if the samples are not very different from each other than VRay can use fewer samples. The **Min samples** control gives you ability to set the minimum number of samples that must be produces before the early termination algorithm begins.

On the **Environment** rollout, make sure **GI Environment** is turned on and color is set to white. Also, make sure **Reflection/refraction environment** is turned on.

Go to the **GI** tab. On the **Irradiance map** rollout, set **Current preset** to **Low**, **Subdivs** to **60**, and **Interp. samples** to **30**. Make sure **Randomize samples** and **Multipass** are checked.

Randomize samples allows you to get rid of artifacts caused by regular sampling. When turned on, the samples are randomly jittered to get rid of the artifacts. **Multipass** allows you to make several passes with progressively finer resolutions starting with **Min rate** and then moving toward **Max rate**. It allows VRay to make better sample distribution in the irradiance map.
On the **Light cache** rollout, set **Subdivs** to **1000**. Turn on **Pre-filter** and **Use for Glossy rays**. Make sure **Filter** is set to **Nearest** and then set **Interp. samples** to **10**.

When the **Pre-filter** option is enabled, the samples in the light cache are filtered before rendering. It ensures a less noisy light cache. In pre-filtering, VRay examines each sample and then modify it so that it represents the average of the given number of nearby samples. When **Use for glossy rays** is on, light cache computes the lighting for the glossy rays as well, in addition to the normal GI rays.

On the **Settings panel | System rollout**, set **Dyn mem limit, mb** to **400**.

Dyn mem limit allows you to set the total RAM limit for the dynamic raycasters. If you set limit to **0**, V-Ray will take as much memory as needed.

Save the render preset with the name **finalPreset**. Take a render by pressing the **F9** key [see Figure 17].

You can replace the **torusGeo** with any geometry and render it using the studio lighting you have just setup.

Note: Check glassMaterial.max
The glassMaterial.max is provided with this eBook. That file uses the lighting setup created in this eBook. Render the glassMaterial.max file to view the results.

Summary

Now, you know how to setup a studio light setup using 3ds Max and VRay. However, this is not the only way to setup the studio lighting. You can use different lights and render settings. I recommend that you experiment with various settings and master the art of creating a studio light setup.

Other Books from Raavi Design

Raavi O'Connor

Build Studio Light Setup
Using
3ds Max and VRay

raavidesign.blogspot.co.uk

Raavi O'Connor

Exploring
Standard Materials
in 3ds Max 2015

raavidesign.blogspot.co.uk

Raavi O'Connor

Create
Backgrounds, Textures, and Maps
In Photoshop
Using Photoshop CC 2014

raavidesign.blogspot.co.uk

Raavi O'Connor

Exploring
Utilities Nodes
In Maya 2016

raavidesign.blogspot.co.uk

b-2   Other Books by Raavi Design